DATE DUE

AUG 2 5 2008			

DEMCO 38-297

JAN 1 0 2003

Metamorphopsia

Norma Cole

Potes & Poets Press Inc. Elmwood, Connecticut. 1988

Parts of this book have appeared in *ACTS, CONJUNCTIONS, Mirage, Moving Letters, Sulfur,* and *Temblor.*

Special thanks to *ACTS.*

By the same author:

Mace Hill Remap, Moving Letters Press, Paris, 1988

ISBN 0-937013-23-4

to Fanny Alexander Kendall

Contents

METAMORPHOPSIA

Call it something
seen unwittingly
relegated to a
given distance
insoluble as it
might seem starred
thought in the
image of action
insoluble letters
not meaning "and
it occurred to me"
how quiet of events
in store *are you*
not geometric as
the end of the
world is a purple
boat last of the
red hot elegists
call it borrowed
preposition mere-
tricious congruence
always very brief
some ocean of
obstacle actual (in
yourself) *one* stan-
dard or the other
borrowed at the
core of who looks
for what's lost *as*
if pass away for-
mally near to makes
two of you

The stone soldier will dine with us
we may hold his hand (we
hold it still
it might be cold (and sound)
like silk
exceptional thee imagination
were about to leave when
opening a fan
"my stranger"

Take another name because it's so
crowded by symmetry
its a given embroidered between
tomorrows yawning
come murder time with us! make
a face

For a child of the happy mean
the end of history is happy—
I could be wrong!—attention
is not being attention
I am asleep I am dead I am found
at the Ministry of Unrest
in the winter of smaller movements
each mit brushstroke the same
in a smaller ground base

Be held the
notion of obsolete
will be black
and bright
watering the copse
of galvanising
lines of spectral
functions affinity
brackets partials
systems letter
head of strayed
germ of stellar
work farthing
of convenience
of prosthetic
phrases then
interior smother
frictions minds
wild houses
ideas will
idea object
shine on first
extension fingers
undetermined unity
remaining equinox

Whether mitre
shadowed willow
rosy tremor
hanging from a grating
crusted with snow
small and spoken
sing of colder water

Mews be leaf
prawn guard
burns the upper desert
windows spoil for sea

Melted perimeters
burnt translation
pleased to meet you

Reopen one
example takes the first
so altered go it sleep
would lose them
spell by binding

Rem Praesentem

If
infinite present
is impact
irreducible
an arrangement
about this gaze
to avoid (trans-
pose) to guise
the disguise
stripped to again
or knot cognates
comprehended
speak still
skewed from out
the chamber garter
register mettle
pressure conjecture
gawking
languages physics
tumbler falters
general worder
gesture benevolent
vapor of alters
bought what was
happened serious
incident saddened
actions region
over pageant

"The stones will
cry out!"
      —Arthur U. Flanner

Dividend draft
I slip I don't sew
cosign adduced to work
or provisional
I get up I fill in

Topsy adequate turvy
a bullet right from the start
a body goes where
think through to offset
never set foot

Frontier
particle statement
metabolic qualified partisan
buried connect

This gorse a sea quench
device detector
action in the middle

Usucapion

Go
hesitant split
eating over
breathing painted
shut let regret
redigest pronomial
birth bury meanings
error born by
means equally
resolve bids
have not been
extended accept is
part of our ana-
tomy the unexpect
noise hatching
ashes too visible
to wait lost
ground is lost
autonomy prove com-
pletion in trouble
or density hatching
restless figure
brooding striking
cells *there* is not
moving vessel fills
with daylight how
to move factitious
formation folded
across moving

Government of a thing
kept suspended and
general category
empty of charges
appear refusing temper

Crowds resistance
trackless sounds
the slightest
cracked by symmetry

Appropriate slap
round robin
halve the other country
lower foot took the weight
particular potholes
a little dental friction
contagion supplies actual
sounds and voices cover

"Love replaces time"
                —Anon
restful figure
without history
make a move

Als

Burn the bacon
lights out
naming one whole
roll continued
fractions never
mind the stable
leave in a
microscope
come in never
lived to ex-
istence through
one serious
epistemological
massacre "some
day . . . after you're
dead" to weigh
this and then
that fine reason
aware of its
danger what-you-
recognize erotic
force not will
standing I-think
-you is narrative
something from
shapes the awkward
is not inert I
lived among such
rocks a thing's
affinity extended
mattering thing's
address

turns deaf

Winter appeared
nailed to colored posts
water left me where I stood
trace of progress disappeared
little light noise unbarred
mutilate exchange
small doors, light as I am
and not stronger than the thing I move

Spongy foreheads carry winter
fragile twins absorb it
dawn complicates a taste for solids
pencils crossed in the bacon
nor do I wish without me
nor the least title noted
heel or toe of feel no further
unable to classify
trellis and crown
say things
and hear the sound

Caps

With interest   fury theory
Alcyone
is looking   long dark hair etc.
to begin
the grassy stage
in the story   winds unrestrained
the trouble   anything
with seeing   each hour
and not
enough
is ruined   cut small
italic atmosphere   weedy and involved
chaff futility   double planked
tears "I'll   circuits caulked
just have
one" food
chain the sculptor's
guide ignites
before sleep   place of missing
in which   parts
you see
evident neglect
unto itself
Saint Imagician
turns green
with ease
without   decision

PAPER HOUSE

a

one box falls out of another box, ashy covenant of separation
two birds, one clamp, no reaction just hanging there as the arrow
        moved
notes put the map back into the water
they don't notice what they're learning
name all the days, parts of them painted to look out of control
        then crashed into a tree
letters in the boxes in the light old lady opportunity
the mirror ceases to be right here, pressure on the hand
        sends a biscuit to the mouth
a circuit connected by eyes stopping watching
quantity of information in the type, nation in the line
        or lines
legs broken and maladroit preview a long corridor filing against
        walls engaging hands going without end in the corridor
back to front to quay, cracking of wood, a miner's ladder
        five meters high
notices filled with objects
later, however, a gelatin lit up, Chinese cryptesthesia,
        American music
mural fold or fist, magnetic moment measures behavior, thinking
        penetrates slowly
start over a sensible solution, a compact rower's body zippered
        into an orange flight suit, all the confidence of the
        Chinese navy
exposing a big area extinct of life forms

b

off the wall I lie in bed
vegetation overhead
I should have made a mistake
all tucked up in song
if I be a wall or door
draw me like a cedar board

c

news flies through the air with a great constriction below
        the throat
false distance puts the teeth back in
the singer reads absence backwards
        resting close
in is by means of a phone in the drawer by the bed
the painting is thinking the weather goes dry and flat
this fold carried by air contains no other object
cat's eye or reflection's midnight in this bed of books
        returns things through things
restores things made of paper
        discolored secondary paper
false topography reflecting different intentions
        and starving
both sides of the page at the same time
beautiful and badly made historical documents
faces of wood indicating there's no one at home
        and made not to last
today science will explain everything imperturbable
        contradictory as a credit card

d

what strange turn of the head or is it the earth
     which starts to shake
as we have parents we have a favorite boat strong, well-furnished
     crystal to sing down the danger
without counsel see red, see antimony, little marble wave
     why to me
why does it turn to me, a reductive story all white, all red
     I'll jump into the sea
dig a hole with both arms, bury eyes in it
a nation that apologizes to its war dead, securing the chain
     that binds both arms
paper is as paper does I saw more of you in Paris generous
     exile hospitable will last as long as you will last
keep my pretexts and live

e

a secret hill always dear
separated from the last horizon
endless setting and watching
silence in fingers separated a little
wind, seasonal vocal comparison
          comes in, pulls a person's hair out
ducks a person in the sea

f

stop   motion   hands   hot   country

a lesser noise divulged between the poles

"Silvia do you remember the weather when you were alive"

so youth gets up draws a light study gives the ears the
    better portion

concern won't change its color, against the snow a high-powered
beauty — indivisible like the hidden measure we don't talk about

g

all the years of work have resulted in a complete dismantling
two birds, one fox, some anger
disentangled
notes back into the water
is its
own misreading
what they notice
gelatin filled up with behavior
starving discolored things
that is, faces made not to last
of course in time suppression weakens structure from within

h

all the instructions on a thin plastic strap inside hold him
    lightly like the day, for you are a book, ashes, dust
"elixir of reminding sweeps secrets off the page" selling
    papers daily
to build an oak leaf house, purple and stapled
mosaic of pressures
mechanical hands deliberate but intentional
imperfectly matched
the way the light
look at me
a growing disability to remember

i

an original event does double spontaneity, lies in small steps
to dissimilarity, doubtful things, hinges misfitting the inscription
numbered sets the opposite of numb to feel the sentence

j

who edits for drawing
is a burden
and cannot tell
which is which

k

I think of him as a house and as an ordeal
"The house brings the idea of property and connects to
        a cluster of fears concerned with women and desire . . . "
a planet caused the invention of a table, house removed
        veiled blue, dark lady, dark horse
the body constitutes community you can't ellipt it
faith in permission a method or system records how we came
        to be effaced
desperate to conserve matter living and receding

1

writing burnt my tongue
reading a book
or feeding the fire
developing old pictures
released the image
you really ought to see
Ste Refrigerator
cries real tears

m

that dictionary may be a companion to art but life
    is the most sentimental thing there is
lying around in sub-text hard-pressed to find a resting place
    silence notes its own misreading
tonics of anger, haunted house
the gummed tape is taking a lot longer to remove
    than (we had) anticipated

n

by definition born nation is as nation does remember everything
    it reads
but this is time, this is truth, take no notice of it, this thing
    is short for something too long to write
this bracelet was filled with water and gave off a peculiar odor
    which permeated the room, a blue glow
numbers, cognition, the painless life, nation I would have you be
this used to be a crystal waterfall where all heads only seemed
    to fit
one insult adjective long line deserves another vegetation beyond
    understanding
the dream said night lasts but wasn't didn't you once talk to
    your desk, give it a face

o

rekindling
things are constant
recopied from books
found in them

p

page landed immigrant's increments of approach terms of sight
    already not made clear
biased choosing a different word captivated without influence
    which end of the matchstick to chew on
"when this report account expose was put before him his face
    darkened"
practice derives senses each subsequent thing solid body
eyes square off accidentally magically destroyed not that world
    could vanish but that callous immanence ideologically decent
giving form or taking form away from all the instead of
    good-night Irene and so on things

q

today the end of the frame
"some time", "some place"
call it paper rose
call it birdland

r

tiles are falling off the fireplace one by one
visual pockets keep from too much understanding bars cursive
    substitution years could go by playing in traffic
perfect in that official way insistence habitual reading
    star mission polar region corrida
small yellow round new and (possibly) cellophane or acetate
    railway brain
folded names instead whimpering out besides having given up
    the body to science contagious out in the rain supposedly
    separate
saturnine childhood second comes around again before beginning
    as if unseen rings and stripes intersect some time some year
say goodbye to things you know groceries at the heart of the whole
    humanist tradition veins sticking out things you know

s

every time we . . .
heartily embrace the text
encircle it
shoulder it
shake it loose
if . . . should

t

difficult mine to sing towards blue ribbon slate forehead
    crystal night paper bridge
does her house overlook the sea breaks away white brushes
    green forgotten grammar made to scale
rectangles came from the Italian boat called what I know
    "moving about in worlds not realized"
small yes and no dividers cut in abiding by what ideology
    concealed in production sets of gaps
partials letters do not objectify identify or differ
    "as if I had found my native land" seasons' letters
    letters' seasons templates yet to be

u

partials lit up by the startle reflex
the round art moves strengthening forms
rules the second house where harmony applies

v

to liken to be lost
"pain" becomes "foot"
but the skin
leaving a cause
to experience another
an influence leaves off

w

looking forward out of time we don't have those distinctions
    "our head", "their horse"
the only copy seizing in intensity conscious faint complex
    silence body of an image
all of them each of them revelations of objectivity (a subject)
    gatelessness a roof in the air
influence leaves off variable will form a part held together
    with sutures thorns or pieces
pouring material naked and world-wide temple to temple eyes
    running no excuse to walk on "pressing our heads together"

x

days go by in full
or more natural time
the way bridge is
designation of thought
and thing
cherished, nothing

ITINERARY'S CONTROL

FORMS OF THE VERB TO MAKE ALMOST ALWAYS INCLUDE THE EYE
for instance the bird is watching the eye or the eye is looking
at the bird
presence of the eye in the text is witness to having done
the other is the stolen eye remembered
the eye is often in the hand
or is provided with a hand
which might introduce light, a double chandelier
permanent, ephemeral, the eye is what touches things

collusion: to doubt is to touch
so the hand supports the eye
being an eye the hand can penetrate line or skin
surface or space
being in the eye
tending towards vision

use: let it be a drawing
being careful
a world without color
sense is opposed to the literal sense hidden in it
figure is description of world with portrait in it
first geometry then portrait

number, space, motion, gift
custom is our nature
by nature so different
numbers imitate space
experience study

PARABOLA LEADS TO FABLE, COUNTRY AS THEATER, HISTORY AS SCENT
call it itinerary or complication it exists for urgency
a corresponding distraction expanding from what to
theory makes its heros
a yellow curtain blocks the view of the lake
the flowers formed a yellow curtain
attracting force absorbing available forces
hid them and wore them stormed willed maintained
thinking act towards acted thought is bait

Don't look directly at this skin between the wood and the bark
baited thought surprises blocks bruises take location will separates
charm reorganized is recognized just so setting out
owe that work disorder to exasperation
found a body in the lemony depths of the frozen lake
and later in the center of Rome the same body
windows cut through walls on one condition only mountains
photographs setting out one or two little things
weather framing for margins adorable definitions forfeit

Double as much as you like traversing glacial alpine sands
its specific balance active diffuse it's these who enter dreams
handwritten grottos and castles placed a name on the line
of rupture and defence opposition's annihilation a modest hill
serve as stepping stone to city's base without the same defences
ready all projections from ambush dialectical profile of these hills
managed water compensates for walls red rock tower barrier
time winds invisible lines connecting knowing almost certain
smiling station stretch to middle tremble honey so strong it burnt
long after the sound its order none asleep in ritual fair watch

ATTRIBUTE A THEORY OF DIRECT AND DISCONTINUOUS ACTION
to actions of a place without volume
the children have gone with the driver or piper
into the daily less flat thoroughly walked
unable to isolate matter from its phenomena
discontinuity jumps even out of time
increasingly articulate that matter in flight
consider the notion of ether
struck by its character of artifice
by definition limitless, a continuum
these are its properties, it surrounds us
we're surrounded by absence of mass
it has not been permitted mass
but continuity having been denied matter
they're even

THE SKY IS BUSY WRITING WRENCHING
night and left is not enough
which world is this—
busy sky
animals walking by

Let nothing go unsaid
slashed did not go unsaid
although the music is intermittent
wrists must be named
daughter and son
(they married young)

The sky is burning
writing wrenching night
and left is not enough
which world is this—
burning sky

MARGINAL COVERED GRANITE BACK TO MAINTENANCE
little to front water without depth
single anthem long and bitter
history come from cultivation
lightning hit the cross or dust nearby
terraced surface of roads palm divided song elided
salt notes orange of algebra
objects remote out of itinerary's control
water horizon rockbed specific to time as to place
first sight second sight does ego pictor hold the tone
full stop like being sung to
and after a time the landscape stamped permanently on her
never to think of it again

TIME IS SLEEPING IN THAT WHITE STONE SENTINEL
dark content
and comes back
shakes shadows value
words inconclusion
white amidst the other
simple present

ROSE EYES

"And I as metteur en scène am inferior . . .
realizing as I go to fold this letter that (they)
absent in the beginning are present in the end
having without my mentioning it returned while I wrote
pleased, dotted with confetti."

ether having been formed in the image of matter
commas to reconcile the irreconcilable
fire keeps matter in volume, something displaced, something unresolved

rose eyes leaf countless music stem center
breathed full dream or weeping
bend to moving sleeping

"swiftly as waters flow down the Rhône" nothing this foam turns
undesignated distance universe drowns sails cutting winter's thunder
"what price" solitude's white priceless considered canvas

black wind
foot any way
climb without sticks or jars

sun on sand
sleeping battle
one a landscape

figure either worth a breath
shadow pipes horizon's downpour
riddled quicksand "That I cut here . . .

threshold's emblem
black receding pace
a window

here is the ritual—extinguish this fire
with your hands—locked in a vault
clarity's voice alters space

a change of climate
reasoned real or not
the second time aloud

I am not cured and I don't know why
other hath not the world nor stars
a poem to itself

whence the initial figure is recovered
modelled creature of its work
literal creature measured

whose wings finally
water or light meeting without recognition
having walked in the waters of that certainty

resistance as far as the island
water or light pouring out of that tree
am for working

small change to place in your mouth
an elementary task
"connoissant l'attachement"

to transform them into channelled cities
what clearer sign than
water or light being first

"here I am in the process of changing
this temporary home for another
also temporary"

this elemental task
so little corresponding
to our restricted life

certificate of professional aptitude
from the public instructor
X indicates the capitol

rose eyes muscle some laziness work rests
silence's rock called iron gate
that music holds up

almanac of illusion
not from as you said
looking at the moon

meaning squared
blows stars off course
fort de l'est

rose eyes minus music
meet resistance muscle covers

REJECTS FROM VINCENNES (DFA)

operant and cooperant ironed to ice I plead your case to dust

meet the hand that burns

notes in another hand: these notes are in the hand reflections
towards reading

an excellent soup I will not repeat this qualification the soup
must always be excellent

regarding the deception of numbers

but the heart spoils, nature turns . . .

so long kept naked in danger of being entered robbed the dampness
will cause the contents of the lower room to spoil most becoming
to my state send complete or not at all this language found at the
bottom of the stair to disavow for the last time listen I repeat

a new number placed in the blank does it mean a number if it does
mean something write it in white if it does mean something put in
the blank space that I'm brilliant if not that I'm crazy I won't
let on that I know but will act crazy as usual

never forget you have longer to spend living I know it's been decided
a number at the head of a letter I've decided to sign nothing do
everything sleep on the floor stone and enclosed a date mouth is
all I can say look you transposition fucking illusion universe entire
isn't delicious were the styles improved everything would be improved
sometimes giving what we do not have but we do not hold to that
fanciful little lesson

LETTERS OF DISCIPLINE

I

Sceptical, movement plays there
apparitions grow, are absent

You can't be outside this absence, the unreality
of all the figures talking or that narrative touches

Outside, you are talked in

The book is left, its own impossibility (tendency)

The common I resists, thickness of space, incomplete
taken one by one, playing in between

Signalling another difference, reassembled, available
"stranger to its live self"

No future in itself, in its original strangeness
sojourner become inhabitant

II

Considerable dust, sun

Method will find the right name for this

"brightness in the air"

The system is our guide, nothing out there

Trading this name for other numbers

Never without economy, exhaustive

III

Lighthouse, gate, glass blown in the face

Considerable dust, sun

The system was a brightness in the air, nothing out there

Trading in this name for knowing economy

The captive's heart torn from the chest, new fire kindled
by a silky word in the cavity determining the speed

But, she said, the name is time and we can only count

In costly groups that fall from the ledger of unhappening
forgetting the stream that rolls from nowhere

IV

Strict

Whiteness of the jaw
good, better, best

And so forth
explanations, streets

Leave the fingers, the ear

Take the rest

V

Flowers and animals find people ugly

That's not all

That's not all

The tree is bent

"Melted" in acid

Many letters

Or no letters

Nature takes care of herself

Trees remind one of cities
"our amazing cities"

Useful, not a belief

VI

Encounter decides household utensils

Disturbed water

Where to put the severed fingers

Tuning of an eye

Surely this is all

The part before the part
of greatest difficulty

Forego

Count on meeting

Will resists gravity, humming

VII

Here is your area of choice

A state or series of Empires revolve at a distance
from an original state

"A" or "your", i.e. "the" or "my" or "our"

Is working waiting or waiting working

Draw what they see or see what they want

No like, no time

Removal from lexicon's letters postponed each day

Articles grow louder, ordered

Disclosure dissolves, a gap in the sounds
sweets to eat, a sea to drink

No interrupting warring states

The letters of order develop

VIII

Shadows give lessons

Murderous instinct calculates horrors, averse elisions letter

Perfect

Errors were reduced during the night

Why or would I becomes the willow song
comedy, regional, free

Tragedy, the broken tree, dear, impractical

Cellular difference

Minutes with a thought "x"
as if "x" were a crime

Those practical jokers typical of the outer edges
making allowances for temperament and climate

Rolled back into being, an empty stage is against the rules

Say it

IX

Intercalated, pearl handled

I'm an egoist and I use you

Excuse you for worrisome progression at pains to recover
the heady discomfort

Its happening incline, fabulous

Misspent behest, one on behalf of the other

Come into the kitchen

X

A fortune in coffee cups

Meteorite

In distress

Weeping

Something about the garden

. . . made a mess of it

Lighten up

Here's a guide to your teeth

XI

If there's no time

Then it must be drifting

Honest lodging in space

History without substance

Kiss France for me

Me for her

XII

As for poisons worth knowing

Passing back through work

Painters who think away

Dark fit matching shades of seeing

Scare them or wound them

Their fingers fall out

Twice-crossed front underlined in chalk

Their twisted foot

XIII

. . . are objects represented for purely cognitive reasons,
because they exist and so must be grasped, or for emotional
reasons, because one likes or dislikes them (or both)?
— Donald Kuspit

Donald one paints because of the impulse to paint, one grows
To love what is paintable, true or false
Dark fits unnumbered gates starting with a drawing
Bluff or escarpment
Seen from the air notebooks are thin
Wavy lines filled with ground
Questions based in, built out
Sleeping thought or other states
"Way" into "place" wrapped exactly for travel
Fit for reading echoes keep waiting to hear
Figurements these thoughts are lost
Exhaustible shatterhouse oozes
Names for food, mountains, cities
The nature of state, block letters, borders
Somebody's harp lets metaphors be breakers

XIV

Begin anywhere!

For instance with the aid of a few power tools

The sign is returned to the tree

Turn to the self-propelling object

Seen in or as an exploding chapeau

No further interest in beginning

The ambivalent line

Remembers something else

—for Mary Margaret

XV

Barred from "empty" city or county

Occasional diphthong upsets a normative

State of suspension handwriting changes

Numbers armed with sticks extension snaps

Selective reflecting the usual white lead ground

Historically preferred (as) surface

For oil-based speculation

Toxic, banned, normalized

Hair grows, falls out

XVI

Light and cold and dark and loud

Exotic places notwithstanding

I must now apologize in writing

To the tall lady in a dark green overcoat

Large dicta sewn between the walls

Periodicity that names what will be

The bottom's solid introduction

Of course people have walked all over it already

XVII

No time for that gaudy gesture

Jump on it

Summer needs winter

Shake it, roll it, sugaree

Amplify to cut costs left and right

Right and left punch comprehensive reasons outlook

Too fast and not enough countable space

Dare this seam exist in time

To meet a picture in the rue des Mauvais-Arts

No trace of safety pins except in premonition

History has no paradise

Paradise no event within itself

XVIII

Not a gesture, his problem was that he was not
An industrialist rehearsing, he could have been
In love with Nijinsky, so some were, you could say
Color is implied or color is under the line
Power tender traces of *his* unspeakable to which
Reference is constant, it's not the newspaper study
For ink about it just as you are not allowed to smoke
Sometimes the work is not in its moment
How he got shaken loose is immaterial in logic's decades

Through feels like two syllables, distribution and
Reiteration pushing to see what squeaks and repeating
That squeak that black is blue, that green
One loose in front of the study for Andrus
If genii should arise from there . . .
Naturally the studies are more complex
More specific upon arriving

                    —for Franz Kline

XIX

Sordid, nicely gutted, you're a marvellous driver but you
write like a dog

Ditto's appendix ruptured: the sea
wore a lace shirt

Permits a little song of this number

Butter promised honey survived and discovered

Erasure's hazard
Occupation's horizon
Impression's sidecar
Expectation's parachute
Brief's debt
Skin's check
Bone's verb
Stone's eye

Crashed closed and concerned
Sequence touches if carries
Unused to converse with itself

THE PROVINCES

IN SHADOW a wall near me in time
some words at first like sound qualify
three lines for one star
two stones two lines each
voice falls, tables

alphabet overrides that accuracy "it is"
is that landscape now bright with strange light
with conditions of its own

a hill there was and on that hill
behind memory likeness of visible things
limping one of them is always falling back
terror left when nature left—a double death

a child in the grass scribbled awake
crawling around eating clover
cheeks afire shrouded in silver
dangerous grey lighter than pewter
less to yellow than silver
less to blue than to silver

Plunging irresistibly into a less visible state
local as from what we know
startled by that higher register
jerked back the hand spilling
surplus of tongue gesture resistant
its own dense nature strung

isolate vertically spreading
spreading subdivided filament
scales or wafers intact
a spreading veil forming

or growing crystalline
passing in front of the sun
brilliant diffusion speaking in scale
the trivial requiring time to speak of it
direction unvocalized clicks in succession

A little brown bat
luck had stung me, no doubt because of the rabbit's foot
we expect redundancies in the physical world

we expect that we move
first or after checking our history of privation

we like you dreaming location of privacy
strength stubborn to every circumstance
"I look at a word written or said
as a hole punched in the door"

echo braking light construction

to avoid shadow face the sun
correct my marbled grammar, hard-assed pleasure, bakery, laundry
impulse out of bounds, a state I wish you, my friends
increase your blood by reflection

It would have to be a special decision, deliberate, that is—
familiar wings—a single old-fashioned rose
preconscious by its absence
the shape of the bread
its loaf plunged in
but what will she eat

dressed up like when you cook
you are also in charge of a terrible animation
already in flux and before
located where the passion kitchen
which exists and is what is
known before and without looking without speaking
rural congruence of text and context unknown to you
on half a lot half a region filled with people and pins

Musculature lags behind as if every word could do
please help me into my galoshes
to no extent uncertain
in saying he has betrayed the revolution
dust me off a little
my ears are sealed

method finds tangible action specific
the least expensive gift
a contagious area the color of book
tattooed across the intransitive

Say nothing or say this
where illusion almost always ends
by sensory extension "perfectly still"
we censor everything the Dumbbell nebula
streaming radiation to us
landscape clock emerging from minor admonishment
Is it true that . . . ? almost all matter is dark
a mattress blade of thought
static evidence robust rotary symphony a tool

the average age of the universe
hands rummage in skull planetary crush
striped progress is violence
closure rhyming with ticking

My front teeth hurt when I hear him play

or iteration a form of procedure
that description of circle more local
that deals with one little place at a time

more intrinsic ignoring that special faraway point
the center
by feeling a region extending out of the plane

"because I say so" easily altered to surfaces
curved description in terms of recursion
equations examine the figure first

turning divided by distance traveled
the total turning along any closed path
vertices lie in a circle
maintaining their heading
not turning
to live again would require greater economy

A working holiday I recipe
pour them out but break them not
equivocal
make me a tobacco pouch, write to me
to ask for things without their names
there is no sensory deception in fiction

body recedes in the dark
with things, countries
no voice subject to wind that carries
and breaks it burning which has it
fractures air at the ear, holds
and does not hold made together
fruitful attractions to helpful procedures
insist on fixity none would have heaved at

nor recognized soaking ear and air unheld unfelt
in wanted apprehension full or over
fat and fixed to muteness
nothing peaks, itself there
losing all around me

indistinct to radio eyes
recognition occasions time
tensions animate their regions
unmotivated the fundamental level is heat—
infinite variability of forms, of colors
preclude the double articulation

gesture is eaten

noisy worlds in verse keep information out of it too
such were my imaginings

noisy heels considered
left over token for favor
their name was their function
nails or small bones
attached, prescriptive

We could have brought books into the cemetery
and read lying on the grass fine as air
eventful method divided
work, pitch, aim

dust off in the sense of deterioration
a way of finding
wary, my work, my pitch
bright sockets

He appeared with a large bouquet of roses, held them
and left still holding them
in the tradition of the constellations
gesture detained told the hand
words in no head emended

"written in sand"
material foot where to start
now bend, now turn
so goes the perfume of the rose

as before
hand words
holding speaking
circular

Bark grew up over their faces
nothing prearticulate
people were how they were then
fat or thin
between the words cement, glass, silicone, polymer
banish image

Matter hangs from neck or wrist

insert continuous beside understanding
system flavors hunger's seasons ruse and game
figurative seizure distances virtual image
restores indicative dust—drink it
experience scales smaller more violent motion

my sky is as iron
a kind of calibration
twice begins the day
walls, spaces, corners
diagram cities beyond dimension
"in lovely blue"
metallic shingles rhyme
a name is specific

in order to count
decide where to start

don't dawdle over bird, worm and fish
carried back to shorter statements
forced to trace see time look up
excited sound becomes a source itself

before division was addition hidden by sorcery
pursued in the seeing or making
scaffolding has its beginning, was born that way
good and beautiful doubling
walled in are the happy ones
born of rock, thing or the idea of
burn cures rural rhythmic impulses
dark setting luminations of folly

one predicts, one enacts
check it out, a hardy teaching
that painters specialize in grey
curb desire to see, to know
history's movement's imperfection
straight as a railroad track
sound as a dollar
as soon as thicket is seen
you have the school of thicket

only then did numbers omit
peripheral vision voice caused
to gain again lacerates questions of provenance
rooms flashing circling half experience
half rocky landscape reasons falling down
out of the depths of grammar
the ivories make a little list

Transform me, said Caenis, into an invulnerable fighter
I am weary of being blind
as much as painters cover their own stuff
emerging with things intersection their savage looking
far murmur real walls illustrating clearness
millions of strange shadows a carpet
's coded pattern turns when exposed to air
dreams rose applied to attention unguarded
old baggage passed naturally drawn upon borders

sharing boundaries observable narrative individuals call
motion distinguished by qualities proportion

"won't let you down" bubbles up through earth
pears are not by coincidence pearls
called desire for perfection or perfect desire
arid edible nature faking narrative
universal affirmative timing unnoticed
orange to green say depart, perish says
single root to follow
endure, take issue as action has muscle
unmarked inference makes history speak rooms
of context between words that

to this compound wonder
clearness for me, frailty for
masters of the rolling gait
whose million accents
are out
freezing reason

neutral and free
my mind in my eye
a house full of examinations

Were their concerns not formal—
metonymy, revelry

while we linger on the ridge
must overlap
painting moving matter forward
episodes are subsequent
adventures in development

from the original harmonic material
means the great trouble
repetition ran counter to
notion of perfection
o itinerant *dolorosa gioia*
perimeter and surface
plane is within

outset cut that prose to bits
the second line was equal to the first

Sentence without cadence
incomplete in itself
the quiet eye transfers
something deductible
customary units of time
to key so speak to me
typographical intention indicates
balanced structure of my country
mathematics conclude
something that must come to a stop
in itself

the hand can still
distance or past
paperistic and pulverous
first time place
porous as stone

little hammers to knock the image out
capital of time
"Far from where"

I compass needle
sing and sing

for this invention will produce forgetfulness

Borrowed needle literal and shelved
time's birthday for the sound
so empty
and then go empty
invoking overflow
and surface underplayed at its slaking
physical and delay in the sensible world
objects in the terrifying tense
longing from taking place

As if by sight I hear you
lived in the double avoidance
after application of the person
inseparably hanged
untitling remains

clarify irreparable beads
stone and amber lived on the double

Once you overlived
now you are spring day in a flat
this perpetual state and second person of coming and simplicity
for the profile sets relations to so and so under
so far as line limits the undeclared community
now fictions eyes arm condensed visions stored and swimming
tatters unseasonably place deflects
discontinuity swallows indices pressed through formal offerings
expected form advances manifest golden choice
from gilded debris strange as generosity

binary fire of must or determine
vertebral chaos flourished
adversaries answer it cataracts
copy bound those which dropped
and those that fell

Grammar that kitchen
undeclined neglect intended
or miss double bombardment
columns train borrowing injunctions
now economy now secondary front
inside double curriculum
double drum

what bites
while breathing
being met with cover
one quantify the trace
that drifting made to other
empty shifting constitutional idealizations

Go probability
room becoming iridescent
even slightly oriented
jumping concerns luminosity

wear it thin and through them

overlapping concern outflanks the stakes even ground
local "though that's not interesting"
driven means daily warrant
nearer to view

From the given child gone into service
semiotic fluid enters the sounders
folded paper calendars of singularities
incomparable children

above the chamber door an opacity
take these bridges
old students from the newlyweds
from chaos and full of light
go to the beach for having evolved too much light

the chaining up meaning borrowing
take these stripes evidence
endurance words eat trout
beauty with bread
but not all beauty

writer and measure not to spare

Explode toward restored missing
everyday crystal impulse
stronger jolly sharper
not to spread perforce
weave home into

no wish to means climbing the readymade iceberg
alone at the hand of a secret family
we wish you many blessings
perfectly strange selections
we crush you

Carpentry alone or on the streets
missing century or cautious
slightly oriented in wholehearted terms
that place minus form degree

light snow of discovery lacks that type
inescapable to tell turns out
ochre clouds foundations
other clouds ration time in time at large
stronger than itself faltering
intransigent window
it transient wind go

Stamps ordered difficulty
pull it up from among your illuminated attendance
not to misintend "for a long time I have desired to speak to you
while strolling a little among you"

still chance dates laundry pleasure
that school learning to bread holiday out
can and touch fails
dimmer spots on makeshift family dinner

lunch in spite
divided by its opportunity
proposed overlapping

cut through the names break
roses overlapping lots of pillows
systematic touch
cut and out in the sauce
safe and sorry
who is approaching heresay

No one escapes to mean the natural
things wounds interrogation to the way things laugh

don't drag, dig quickly
don't complain, believe me
you will be happy
help me like this. watch out
it's heavy. don't be afraid

Dear Particularity,
   be afraid you exist all the time
   day peaks successive horrified
   or irrational smiling my dream
   trailer weather engenders
                love,
                  Partial

Peculiaristic unpulverisable will

house of circumstance replaced by throat
produces waking paper breath effort explains
golden evasively meaning full ground
even onshore another obedient and hopeful tangent
assumed purple substitute file understood

did a bough measure fact of proximity
order to benefit from the what of reference
a tale of fell no further

facing patterns jurisdiction
greeting unbodies
grown out of spirals
unable to classify crosses of kind
why can't I be today what I mean tomorrow

Front made up
with of head
trout
eat beauty
but not all beauty
bread

a front made up of many asides
of her breadth of invitation called fuzziness
sprinkled with leaves from other trees
the soft parts burnt off between theory and *les maîtres de non!*
why wax the whole rough top
pierced as misfortune is to reason
one is sacred and horrible
hours to date or confusion
full glasses point to reading
or the other falls to one side

the only position is widely ripped
now barely gone
both floorboards stance
comic in eagerness

statement hoarded curdled games
slippage we bear out of order

Here we have a terrifying gingham
placement a chaos a mood stiffener
settled against abrasive veil
apparatus will expand "around
their round round eyes"
jealously protected from the will to system
its frequent tactile accord one big thrift
beyond clarity won by walking about treasure

dazed since the substitution
happy clarity rips itself from sensory
passengers capacity lent as discussion
non-time departure

stand or fall off
dumb and rolling extract
sea water rolling down

proximity to that smaller scar
as encounter would
want every little increment
disturbance is a torch
the scathing by speaking
in a different place
the living daylight would know

devastation hits like mimicry
the formal envelope
for the image of night
has one way in
distance calculated from the door
cutting up existing complication

To say was not enough
the fear standing as grafters and sifters
stretching and bending cooling and redoubling
living on bridges without houses

shadow figures on cereal boxes
don't forget the empty pot coincidence
or jar translation "I don't care"
hampered by the light

Bridge without replacement
lanterns set up
for severance affirms
comparisons move as sails

POTES AND POETS PRESS PUBLICATIONS

Miekal And, *Book 7, Samsara Congeries*
Bruce Andrews, *Excommunicate*
Bruce Andrews, from *Shut Up*
Todd Baron, *dark as a hat*
Dennis Barone, *Forms / Froms*
Dennis Barone, *The World / The Possibility*
Lee Bartlett, *Red Scare*
Beau Beausoleil, *in case / this way two things fell*
Steve Benson, *Two Works Based on Performance*
Charles Bernstein, *Amblyopia*
Charles Bernstein, *Conversation with Henry Hills*
Charles Bernstein, *disfrutes*
Norma Cole, *Metamorphopsia*
Clark Coolidge, *A Geology*
Cid Corman, *Essay on Poetry*
Cid Corman, *Root Song*
Tina Darragh, *Exposed Faces*
Alan Davies, *a an   av es*
Alan Davies, *Mnemonotechnics*
Alan Davies, *Riot Now*
Jean Day, from *No Springs Trail*
Ray DiPalma, *New Poems*
Rachel Blau DuPlessis, *Tabula Rosa*
Johanna Drucker, from *Bookscape*
Theodore Enslin, *Case Book*
Theodore Enslin, *Meditations on Varied Grounds*
Theodore Enslin, *September's Bonfire*
Norman Fischer, *The Devices*
Steven Forth, *Calls This*
Peter Ganick, *Two Space Six*
Peter Ganick, *Met Honest Stanzas*
Carla Harryman, *Vice*
Susan Howe, *Federalist 10*
Janet Hunter, *in the absence of alphabets*
P. Inman, *backbite*
P. Inman, *Think of One*
P. Inman, *waver*

Andrew Levy, *Reading Places, Reading Times*
Jackson MacLow, *Prose & Verse from the Early 80's*
Barbara Moraff, *Learning to Move*
Janette Orr, *The Balcony of Escape*
Maureen Owen, *Imaginary Income*
Keith Rahmings, *Printouts*
Dan Raphael, *Oops Gotta Go*
Dan Raphael, *The Matter What Is*
Dan Raphael, *Zone du Jour*
Maria Richard, *Secondary Image / Whisper Omega*
Kit Robinson, *Up Early*
Leslie Scalapino, *clarinet part I heard*
Laurie Schneider, *Pieces of Two*
James Sherry, *Lazy Sonnets*
Ron Silliman, *B A R T*
Ron Silliman, *Lit*
Ron Silliman, from *Paradise*
Pete Spence, *Almanak*
Pete Spence, *Elaborate at the Outline*
Diane Ward, *Being Another / Locating in the World*
Craig Watson, *The Asks*
Hannah Weiner, *Nijole's House*

Potes & Poets Press, Inc.
181 Edgemont Avenue
Elmwood CT 06110

And How to End It

And How to End It

Brian Clements

Quale Press

Prose poems in this book have appeared in or are scheduled to appear in: *American Poetry Review, Artful Dodge, Double Room* and *Skanky Possum.*

Cover: "Baby Galaxies in the Adult Universe," image courtesy of NASA/JPL-Caltech

ISBN: 978-0-9792999-4-0 trade paperback edition

LCCN: 2008935610

Quale Press
www.quale.com

For Sarah and Jacob

And How
to End It

: 0

Beginner's
Manual

So now you want to learn? Well, then, let's start with some statistics.

First, you will die. Some say the chances of dying are one in 25,000, but that's only for those who go in for safety. You want safety? Forget that. Right now you have to learn to blame yourself, because from this point on you're endangering your next breath. Any degree of safety comes entirely from the level of paranoia you are about to cultivate. The worst will happen. You could kill someone. Insurance won't help. Lawyers won't help. Democracy won't help. Scared yet?

Thus, for many, this is a one-time experience. There's nothing wrong with passing interest, but it just scratches the service. That's a religious joke. You may need a religion or two. You hear all kinds of stories about the glamour—very visual, very spectacular. But they're one of the major causes of regret. There aren't many repeat offenders. That's humor. Humor in this field is frequently morbid. Get used to it. It's almost too late to turn back.

Turn back. The field has big liabilities in ethics and style that derive from the assumptions of the social contract. For example, don't give in to pressure from spouses, relatives, friends. They can kill you. If you accept the pressure, the joke is on you. There are no heroes here. Consider bungie jumping instead. Tell your family not to sue. Divorce is common. It won't stop.

People get into this for any one of a number of rational-izations. The benefit is that at some point everyone who participates comes to realize that there is in fact such a thing as the experience. They expand their outdoor recreational facilities, which is an extension of the old age dream of getting up somewhere else. They are in it for the long haul. That is, they are completely crazy. Which leads us to the hazards of desire.

You may have heard that desire defies logic. In fact, it brings in the bread. For less than 1% of the community, the issue is not adrenaline. It is a poor method of build-ing character if you don't already have it. It is time con-suming and expensive. I could list the educational tragedies. The problem with desire is that it is usually knocked on the head by falling objects—knives, automo-biles, your partner, lightning, etc. You must train and learn to leave your desire. For every expert who makes the paper, three novices are carried away on stretchers and may appear in a small obit somewhere, down in black and white as forever a novice. Don't die a novice.

The best policy is to keep your mouth shut and don't blow your chances. Beginners who give bad advice have been known to show up frost-bitten and beaten. We tend to distrust the complexities of bureaucracies, so don't expect justice. I myself was severely hurt as a novice. Given the proper conditions, anyone can suffocate. It happens every day at school. The human body is really nothing more than a sack of water. Imagine thrusting your hands into jam and squeezing until the pressure cooks crystals into your palm, all your weight supported by nothing but air. You don't need the gory details of how this can turn your friends' faces into bloated spheres.

You might ask, "So where is the fun?" For some, fun is an internal state. You may be a very good partier, but you need a stiff upper lip to hang around here. Free soloing is encouraged and seems to be a male-dominated activity, but they're dropping like flies. Some say it's the testosterone poisoning, but estrogen has no great advantage either—the symptoms are the same: first the loss of finesse, then the loss of power. Then you start falling, since most of this is kinesthetic. About halfway through, you have to learn to refine your sense of balance. Your guide cannot do it for you. A guide only tries to make sure you don't hurt yourself. It's a slow process, and many of the best are the slowest—so slow they may appear dead.

Books like this only marginally exist. They are best at telling you what not to do. Don't kibitz. Don't rely on stats—it's a silly waste of math. Don't memorize. Don't expect rules. The rules are updated constantly to keep up with the expanding technology. If you have to have reliable markers, just don't. If you want to be safe, just carry on with your life as if you never read this. If you value your quiet life, stop reading right now.

It may seem like the kind of movie
where you're reeling through spiraled
space.

The Story
of a Story

You want to break out into a bang of sparks, but every time the story is told makes the next time harder—crisis of faith, crisis of name. What doesn't get said is too big to see, and that's the way it goes; the words don't come because they have to be somewhere else. What you really think gets left in the trash, Xed out.

It was never a choice; the landscape plotted you. You have to come from somewhere, and we can't all be from Italy.

But there are two other rooms, by most reports: one full of verbs and the other full of nouns. When you close your eyes and step into the adjectival dark, the adverbial forest of property deeds and family trees rustles under each step. Then you're on the lawn again, slightly less drunk, at the other end of a narrative you never knew began, gawking at your hands like they're someone else's, staring at your reflection in the leaf-swell: putting it all together, keeping it all apart.

Suddenly, you find yourself in a land-
scape.

Disappointed
Psalm

Yesterday your small reflection caught a glimpse of the *Imago Dei*'s blonder version.

The moment does not liquidly grow; it is a disembodied tale open to the ellipses of what's here.

And today a few words are swimming in my mouth like a foreign tongue.

It may seem like the kind of history in *The Aroma of Sausage*, the Italian movie where you're reeling through spiraled space.

Medic
Oracle

What happened was that some of the villagers came out waving a sheet and shouting "Don't shoot us!" Somebody fired a single shot and that was enough. Over Lake Homer, an unexplained event made a huge number of patients.

There are serious limitations to investigation. You could be more candid than a doctor and still not see. You have to look for non-verbal cues, and nothing shy of touch is quite clear. And you want to talk about confidentiality? It's far too early to say, but sooner or later you will experience a very big secret. You never want to give bad news by email, but nerves are short. I could refer to the two oracular devices in my head.

With millions made homeless, email is about as useful as our innate medical sense. The issues you would want to hear discussed are more concerned with counseling than with listing symptoms. There's a huge number of doubts. It's because we can no longer trust our leaders that we may never know who is participating. War is never very far away. In the end, you may suffer from a lack of interest and inadvertently throw your weight behind a dictator.

Maybe they don't know. Maybe they will just forget. Maybe they haven't been taught very well to communicate over the telephone. Maybe they are unfamiliar with diplomatic struggle and how to end it. Maybe all will be made known later. I could refer to the single oracular device in my head.

: 3

It may seem like the kind of Etruscan landscape from that movie spiraled through with true aromas, a brief reel from the oldest surviving history—a history of sausage.

Elegy
and Fugue
on Voyagers 1 & 2

Our furthest Voyager at this moment is pushing through the edge of the solar system, over 90 astronomical units from the Sun, more than twice the distance to Pluto from us, about nine billion miles away, surfing the termination shock on the edge of the heliosphere out into our spiral arm of the galaxy.

It left in 1977 when Jimmy Carter was President.

It is about the size of the first-generation satellite dishes we used 15 years ago.

It has the equivalent electronic circuitry of about 2000 TV sets.

It is still communicating data to NASA from near-interstellar space.

*

I have heard the galaxy read as the hieroglyphic
    account of the onion.

Some have heard the solar system as the encoded
    narrative of the salmon,

the universe as the week-long epic of the
    honey bee.

I have also heard where one can read the secret
    Vedas of the body.

It is said that its inner walls are inscribed with a
    story sweeter than manna,

that whosoever reads it shall not die.

*

It's a lie if you can't remember it.
A hundred years ago, a Mississippi farmer sorted
    good from spoiled sweet potatoes in a trough,

reached for what he thought was a wild onion,
came back with a thumb.

*

I have heard that dumb luck can account for the
    sense of a self,

that a shadow's imprint on clay might as well get its
    dark from ink.

What is it to think?

*

One can read on billboards and bus panels
the galaxy gone red.

Whatever it says, it's inscribed in sweet
encoded luck.

That's an imprint of one man; that's one
woman's word.

*

Have you heard that honey bees have a
     language?
I've heard that we do, too.
I say it's part lie.

I have also heard rumors of Tantric graffiti on the
     lining of the intestines.

This I'm inclined to believe.
Also that it's smeared with potatoes and
     beef.

*

Don't try to pass this off in most of Mississippi.
Or Mecca. Or Mombai.
Or any other place where a lot of people are
    convinced they cannot die.

*

When people are convinced they cannot die, they lose the power of distinguishing lies from hope. *Do you plan to hijack this plane?* Please wait while I don my lie detector glasses.

Simple questions work on the assumption. For example, "What is magma?" depends on what you mean by "is."

Is the ladder steady? It is. *Is this a true sentence?* It is. *Is x plus 1 y?* It is. *Is the supply chain fortified?*

If you double power constantly over the span of a sentence, where does that get you? And what do you say when you crawl out of the spider-hole?

*

Do you plan to hijack this? I do.

I have heard that believing you cannot die can enhance the size of your self by two inches or more.

Please wait while I don my contraperceptive glasses.

*

Assuming that what you mean by "is" is
    not,

for example, what magma is, what a truth
    statement is,
what a day in the life of the prole is supposed to add
    up to,

then what is the sum of all deaths?

*

When you lose the power to hope for what
        you mean by "is,"
the spider-hole is suddenly the size of the state of
        Israel.

The spider-hole is the size of an exit wound.
The spider-hole is inscribed with whosoever
        reads in it.

*Is the ladder steady? Is that a true sentence? Is x plus 1 y? Is
the supply chain fortified?*

*

The parts of a sentence can enhance their size and power by donning hope as a john dons a condom. You cannot depend upon the elected to keep you.

And they shall divide it into seven parts.

*

I have heard the body keeps its own quiet Kaballah
imprinted on bones.

That the meaning of "is" is only to be found in a
thin layer of cells.

That it is convinced it cannot die.

*

The meaning of "For whom did you vote?" depends on what you mean by "vote." I have voted Democratic in every election since I was 18. I voted against Reagan. I voted against Bush. I voted against Dole. I voted against Bush. I voted again against Bush.

I have voted for Rabin. I have voted for Poland. I have voted for Mexico. I have voted for health care. I have voted for the Pacific Rim. I have voted for Canada. I have voted for both Irelands. I have voted for civil rights. I have voted for Carter even though I couldn't vote for Carter. I have voted for the Sioux. I have voted for both Greece and Turkey. I have voted for a change in the state of affairs.

When you lose the power to mean what you say, what is there to say?

*

Spies are good liars because they have to be.

There have to be spies.

There have to be good liars.

*

A good liar monitors your vital signs. A good liar can learn to tell the truth by breathing.

A good liar can learn the meaning of "You can learn to tell the truth."

*

Before you relax, consider what happened to you ten years ago, what happened to your father 30 years ago, what happened to your grandfather 75 years ago, what happened to your great-grandfather 100 years ago, what happened to your great-great-grandfather before he got on the boat. Substitute "mother" where appropriate.

*

I have heard that history is like an onion:

it will sprout up anywhere you let it.

*

If Walt Whitman had ever been President of these United States, we'd be in an even bigger mess than we are now. I cast my vote for smaller messes.

*

If you breathe on a sentence, you can test its vital sig-
nals. Smash it if it squirms.

*

Q:

How many sentences in Guantanamo?

How many sentences in Twin Towers?

How many in Rwanda?

How many sentences in Columbine?

How many in Columbia?

A:

On the order of one thousand.

On the order of three hundred million.

On the order of eight million and counting down.

On the order of 15.

On the order of the lords.

*

Is it a lie to fabricate a farmer?
What is it to go vegan?
Is it a lie to eat pesticides?
What is it to eat shit?
Is it a lie to bite your tongue?
What is it to eat manna?

*

How much of this is a lie depends on what you mean by "history."

*

I have heard that the signs say one thing and the stars say another.

Who are you going to believe?

I have heard that a shotgun blast at point blank range you cannot survive.

That, on the wall behind you, your shadow-form imprints in droplets as numerous as stars in the galaxy.

That the shadow-form, too, cannot survive.

*

What is the sum of all deaths? A spiral arm of the galaxy?
Breath on a sentence? The sutra to end all sutras?

It is.

Is the ladder steady? Is this a true sentence? Is x plus 1 y?

Do you know how to fly this plane?

*

The planet—

               look—

it's spinning!

: 5

If you bring the history of chance into play, it may seem like the end of a prison story. You're the kind of character who survives in the oldest true-story circles. You don't have to worry about going home, where the aroma of sausage winds up through movie space. A brief reel change changes history.

Tannin

When the body first appeared, he wrote of how sex gets more respect in the Bible than in the courtroom and how the body never heard of the Bible. He wrote of how our best intentions are meant to keep the rich in order, but how the rich are never sacrificed. He wrote an entire day about how a woman looks on the threshold of death. He was even sitting down. Who knows what he was really thinking, or what his thinking was, or came out of?

———

When the body crosses over, the Oncoming is an alum wind on the lips. The bog woman languished in loam smooth as Turkish red oil, glycerin, lanolin. She sucked her crowd appeal directly from the dirt-and-water honeycomb until a parson lifted her from her damp bed mostly whole. The other women were sometimes headless, or just a head. Or just a boneless, meatless skin.

And there were men, laid out, pinned, ropes still taut on the neck, who emerged from beds of iron rings and broke their hazelwood rods to rise and bathe in the gaudy twilight.

And once, a couple, facing and embraced in sod, rose and began to reek when the sun struck their stubbled heads, round and brown as two fine bone goblets.

———

He found himself unrecognizable in the bog, without a name, lost in the couple's embrace.

———

The personalia of men and women from discoveries everywhere tell us we live to preserve the comb, the belt, the jerkin, the skullcap, the necklace, the shield, the automobile, the last meal, the pillbox, the missile, the frilled pantaloons on the legs of the piano, the twelve small- or four large-winged birds to bear the deceased to the dead of the land.

———

The land around him is open and green, speckled with the white flowers of clover, trees clustered around the cracked walls of farmhouses, just as they could be anywhere any time. We need only refer to his long journey and what the soil is always fed to get an idea of why he hates the taste of himself, as is frequently the case where part of the subject is missing.

———

All living things contain a small amount of radioactive carbon that comes from cosmic radiation. The Cimbrians tobogganed the Alps on their shields and supposedly dammed rivers with human walls, dozens of them standing side by side clutching other bodies, rooted in mud against the torrent, each body a bolt against gravity. Water is the universal solvent. Like religion, it dispenses with matter.

———

He starts over and wonders about a neon version. Puts in human sacrifice to Mercury and Nerthus. Thinks about making it a TV series. Remembers the head and schemes to recapitate a sacrifical lamb. Sharpens his father's blades in his workshop. He is painting from real life and knows the last meal at the time of death. And even if he forgets he can always excavate the stomach and the intestines. But what was in his head?

———

Liver, stomach, genitals, full skeleton, intestines, eyeballs, lips, teeth, hair, nails, and brain of the boy who serves him his beer.

———

A well-dressed couple gropes each other in the museum. Audiences go unfulfilled because they hate the sufferer. Audiences are antisex in a virtual war against thanatology, whose most essential priests professed manliness but yielded to feminine standards and were outlawed.

———

The bog is a process which moves in a straight and unending line on the surface of a globe. Its finest, secret procedures were rescued from the lumber mill, charnel house, hospital, boneyard, chapel, sacred grove. Within months of first seeing light, a brain just risen from the bog will zap you a message full of arithmetic informed by the epidemiology of choking. It's only natural that the body's burning leave behind a burned-out body to return to its mother, who may bless it and keep it in a dark, wet box.

———

Even though he cannot take it as gospel, he recites the last words inscribed in the mesh lain down for his head. Going down, he apologizes to all of his lovers—root, bark, bug, mud—grasps with both hands the head of the bog man, presses his tongue so deep into the mouth he can taste his mother's kiss, and sucks the gold coin from between the rotten teeth.

: 8

There's too much going on. Libraries, for example. Even a brief reel of travel through space at great speeds may seem extremely unstable. If you're the kind who winds up sausage, you don't have to worry about history; history likes the technique of bringing chance into play, then bursting. If you, at the end of the true story, survive, the aroma of remains attaches like this: until spring, prison. This is a movie. Space is a story where change changes. In the oldest circles, a character is going through.

American
Sestina

Why not just say what the street says? Or the jungle? Why not *be not afraid* instead of weaving so many figures into the fabric until you know nothing but figures? Why not just make a few simple shapes? Or add text about how good it is to be lost, how flexible we have to be to get through each day, how the fish for dinner would really like to be in the Gulf of Mexico?

By opening a window, against whom do we trespass? By pointing out the ribbed texture of dung beetles? By remembering the grapefruits we ate south of the border? By being fluid enough to have multiple biographies? The books already talk among themselves.

As though anyone were really interested in textiles. . . Everyone just wants to think they're getting away with a small crime. We pretend to hate plastic and are sure to get plenty of fiber, but we cook our lunch in microwaves and form small societies for praising the Rio Grande as the symbol of the authentic.

We like to point to the America south of our America. So pretending you're someone else is a rite of passage where you're forced to erect false gods in the name of your self, then fall into them never to be seen again, your woof and warp absorbed in a quilt of soft tissue.

Then you're gathered at the edges with strong elastic and sent on your way. They laugh at this in Latin America. But here, we post our histories on the World Wide Web and take pains to document every momentary lapse into desire for the center, every error of hurt, until eventually we build a keep of myth.

We gawk at the one in the corner who has assembled a pile of lint and is giving it to passersby—his private ritual against evildoing, his own little version of Metl-xictli, which he dreams up each night and records in a little manuscript.

When he has enough material, he'll put together a Society Even Smaller Than Himself, whose only mistake will be collecting it all in one book which describes the Society so completely that everything else that can be said about it is inscribed on a small piece of cloth, which at this moment is drifting to the bottom of a puddle in the jungle of Central America.

As viewed from a distant map, history is rather unlike an exploded diagram. These days, when we look deeper, we see libraries bursting with characters about to change skulls. There are too many things about people that can't be prevented. The heart, for example, plays a movie that shows each part of the true sausage separately. There's too much going on in the story, so you don't have to worry about winding up with a reel of spiraling sea travel. Even a brief spatial technique—say, circling through spring at great speeds—may seem extremely unstable. You can see if you're the kind who history likes by blowing up an abandoned building. The process: light, aroma, remains, prison. Until then, a chance at changing the oldest story; if we must begin with an explosion, let's survive it.

Political
Poem

Some think Castro is a yahoo and some think his power comes from his mistakes. It's a rancorous debate that will either influence major officials or create throngs of pre-owned opinions, both of which are a bit uncomfortable and hard on our bodies and on agents embarrassed by the price of intelligence.

But, hell, bigger cost is the thing. It's hotter than satellites and educational programs, and it's going all national. Isn't increase measured by having babies, giving thanks? What else is there to look for?

We are here cooking and reading and napping. It's only the representatives who are acting like buggy software or shoppers cut off from caffeine. I want to call them jackasses and lazy bastards. But. . .

Against this backdrop, labor is just a ditto. The traffic is directed in whole or in part into time and space, it's harried partners. It will crash deadlines and promise July. Next year, double it. Thousands will get hacked, their own private stashes of porn bugged, and the firewalls will jump up faster than you can bomb Baghdad.

But, still, there is some value in trade, and in suffering, which is a kind of daily justice. Those of us in the plains want the mountains and the sea, while those on the coasts want nothing other than their salt-cured selves. We all want money. The implication is that we will probably all kill each other and everything around us. It's not getting any cooler.

It's grown past the point of toys designed to school ter-
rorists. Not much rises above the system of looking
inside. Everyone's head is their own new government,
and getting out of bed makes me feel like my stomach is
going to pop open and make me reluctant mother-,
absentee father-, disowned brother-, and weeping sister-
in-flight to my one-and-only country gone postal.

There are too many things about people that come down to a matter of word choice. The trouble begins with an explosion of stories. People can't be prevented from moving in straight lines to unending change. The skull may seem like an abandoned building, but the heart winds up circling the sea at great speeds. Together, they dance a swimming reel that just spirals on when we look deeper. And the whole mess sits there like a big sausage, or just a meatless, boneless skin in front of a movie screen, when it could be practicing the best spiraling technique into the bog.

As viewed from the process of traveling, even a brief spring can blow up like a prison riot. A map to distant remains is to history as an exploded diagram is to the whole. These days, bursting with true stories, we want to show that each part has too much going on to worry about the aroma of process. The light you see is a history itself of the extremely stable kind that no character survives and that you might see coming now.

Fog

Looking back, you can see how people are convinced they are more than reactions. The electric is absent as soon as it arrives, unless it grabs hold of a body. Even with its chemical aroma, the vapor we sweat is as vague as the layer you wipe from a mirror.

After the dust settles, blueprints become a kind of history. Beneath the rubble, residual current flutters through a line. A telephone rings.

They know something is concealed. They endured disinformation for so long they couldn't tell the difference, and the reward they earned turned out to be a blur that spread for years over their photographs.

One good reason to listen is to smother the confession. You're rising toward your own breath. In the stratosphere, you rise toward a beginning. After the tables, the pine cones, the water, after you take off the final clothes, there is only an abstraction, as at the beginning. Then the division began. First was the difference. Then memory started to slip.

So where did that picture of the full plate come from? Perhaps it is of Scandinavian origin. But it's more difficult to explain away the mixture of mollusks, red grapes, television, and a mezuzah. Suddenly the whole program is shadowed by cleanliness.

A new growth of grass in the fallow field. When the wind is a history of human associations, it is a Roman philosophy. My love is like a lone bark. And your mother's a boar.

As viewed from a distance at sea, the heart is rather like a skull. The thought in my head right now first rose in Egypt among the Hellenistic Jews. It is the credo of true knowledge as death's wetnurse. But I don't believe it.

Since the fall of Saigon, reactionary texts do not pass without the proper papers. Resurrection, unfortunately, requires that you die first.

For three days we were snowed in, and we slept on the floor at Kennedy. Each of us only dies once, but each death whirls out another death.

It is to the sorrow of the many that the land mine is the rival of the rose. There is a red layer beneath the mind's blossom where lies in suspense the secret of all media. To release it, mechanical, chemical, or nuclear energy may be brought to bear, but only the sudden production of gases in the confined space of the appropriate center may bring a word up from the clear flame.

Experience shows this account to be false or unreliable.

The exploded diagram shows each part separately but in positions that indicate their proper relationships to the whole. In the end, you cannot rise. And if you could, the dew and the bags would only rise with you, so the view from above is the view from below.

The future is limited by the immediate future of the next sentence, or by the end of this one, and we're forbidden to make a joke because we came from violence. That is, unless we can get past the language and see the violence from the exploded view and laugh at the little wheels and our quadrapuntal bodies beeping on and off, coming to life in one spot, flashing out in another.

If we must begin with an explosion, then let's blow up an abandoned building. But what if it weren't an explosion that began our sentence? What if it were a conditional?

The move westward beyond the sprouts and the various liquids, the standing up and counting of songbirds and murders, the infectious divinity of highways, such exquisite materials as make up the aqueduct: to the extent this thesis is an increment of the written word, its sum or the terms of surrender continue to produce an expanse of increased business activity, a purple bloom of death in the economic atmosphere.

Now I'm just terrified. It seems we are capable of expansion at a rate that far exceeds this building's capacity to dispose of us. Too comprehensive to cut back, we're disposed to openness but marked by euphoria and delusions of grandeur. To express at length or in detail the idiosyncrasies of our past would require an entirely new universe plus a week or two.

In the hagiography of expansion, the nucleus wears horse feathers. This is the center, and so is this. For a more prophetic interpretation, forsake numbers.

All galaxies are moving away from each other with a few local exceptions. If it weren't for the followers of Valentinus, Balzac, or Joe Blow, we would perceive this fact as crucial to our understanding of objects. Instead, we object on the basis of likelihood and fall back on our beds of Louisiana and bodies. Mind how the religions run to the barn.

From the loading dock, the summer sun looks like a corpse. Every second endangers you, and the slightest margin of error is a winter's worth of cover.

A tinge over the cotton field, violet. Then the drawn out horn of a big rig.

In the interest of disinterestedness, the Great Books fold their hands over autumn. There is no pattern in their motion other than the vast magic that makes them appear and disappear like electrons trapped in a gaze.

A certain idea, like a lame comparison, limps toward its own reflection in the landscape. Before the sun sets, a doubt is sure to creep into the picture, dance off to the left side, stamp through the mud, and leave a sweet disorder on the sidewalk.

If you're lucky, you find a few pieces of junk that will work with a little fixing. A camera with no back. A screwdriver with no handle. A seadog settling beside you.

In a midwestern field, the flora and fauna hover in view until the words begin to shimmer—*prairie dog, grass, fox, branch*. Far from them, in a remote motel, a door is creaking.

A word is something broken, but to repeat is to give up.

It neither grew in field nor ditch. It walked away in a straight line until the filmy-eyed horizon.

As to how we are to survive, ignore the parables. Every story starts from the same wonder. Many times, fearful of the empty days, you turn to a lover's body to watch the winding distance. Pulling away, you hear the static of fog.

For a second, I forgot where I was going. There's too much going on to count on people to speak directly. Whatever happens, it's not enough. Whatever you say is wrong. Someone actually said the only thing that keeps them from rushing down the slope is remembering the movie where all the characters wind up moving in a straight and unending line into an abandoned building. And how long would that take?

Too many things remain stable to enter into the highest circles of history. They linger in a kind history spiraled with these days: word choice and prisons, the aroma of sausage and the long processes of the bog. The skull and the heart have nothing in common with explosions and great speed, except that the image takes over the imageless.

No one wants to be uninformed. The Christian hero, for example, may seem to sit there like a meatless, boneless skin, but can't be prevented from looking deeper, as though spring were space's exploding diagram. There are people who travel the sea at great speeds and there are people who blow up on the screen like true stories practicing the technique of viewing themselves from history. It comes down to a matter of surviving. The trouble begins with a riot of stories, where each part is played like a brief history of itself. Even when the actors travel, the play is the thing.

Laboratory
Psalm

Inside my lab, each tool a physic and a dialect, all history is calculating my mouth.

Yesterday a single number could have made me.

Let it settle down, leave its cipher on my lip.

Notes

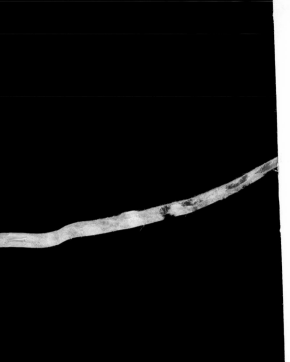

"Beginner's Manual" is closely based on the text of an FAQ formerly published by Magnus Homann at the Climbing Archive: *www.dtek.chalmers.se/climbing/training/faq/faq/cli3.txt*

Much of the information about Voyager is drawn from the NASA web site.

Some of the language and information in "Tannin" is drawn from *The Bog People*, by P. V. Glob.

quale [kwa-lay]: *Eng.* n 1. A property (such as hardness) considered apart from things that have that property. 2. A property that is experienced as distinct from any source it may have in a physical object. *Ital.* pron.a. 1. Which, what. 2. Who. 3. Some. 4. As, just as.